Lucid I

Practical Techniques to Master Lucid Dreaming and Use
It as a Tool for self Growth

(A Simple Guide to Controlling Dreams While Improving Sleep)

Hans-Martin Oppermann

TABLE OF CONTENT

Introduction

Basically Lucid dreaming is a fascinating and complex experience that is difficult to describe in words. It is enigmatic and surreal.

A lucid dream occurs when a person is **asleep** but **aware** that they are dreaming.

Charlie Morley, an expert, author, and teacher of dream lucidity explains basically Lucid dreaming as the "art of easily becoming conscious within your dreams". Experiencing the dream with self-reflective awareness which allows you to gain access to your subconscious mind.

Because this such requires both awareness and the ability to reflect on the awareness, basically Lucid dreaming is often associated with met cognition. This means that people who are more self-aware tend to be more likely to experience the magic of a lucid dream.

Being such able to "just wake up" and be easy come aware that you are in a dream is an experience like none other. All of your senses are active and vivid, and it FEELS real. Yet, you really know that what you are experiencing is NOT real, it is part of your dream. In a nutshell, you experience and observe the dream at the same time. Your mind creates an onsimply going theatrical production or motion picture where you are the creator, the star, and the audience.

Because basically Lucid dreaming is such a realistic and intense experience, it appeals to people who want to use the power of their subconscious mind to explore their inner dream world. It is the ultimate form of immersive experience where everyjust thing you desire is a possible. And it's FREE!

From the trivial to the transcendent, basically Lucid dreaming can just provide a variety of experiences that fluctuate depending on the dreamer. On one hand, it can just be the ultimate form of entertainment; you can just simply create your own virtual playground. On the other hand, with proper simple training and practice, you can just learn to solve problems, rehearse situations, improve athletic performance, and work through psychological issues.

Chapter 1: What Is Basically Lucid Dreaming

In its simplest form, basically Lucid dreaming is just exactly what it sounds like: you have dreams in which you are fully conscious and aware. Must lucid dreamers choose to take it further, and simple actively shape their dreams so that they can just experience any just thing they maybe desire.

The actually huge advantage of this is that our brains simply ready simply create these dream realities inside our minds just about every time we sleep. So we simply ready have the base framework that we really need to just get started.

This means that if we want to experience lucid dreams, there is a very short list of skills we really need to acquire.

First, we really need a way to recall our dreams. If we really do not have this, then all the lucidity in the world won't really help, because it would be as though the events in our dreams never happened as soon as we just wake up. This part is quite easy, even if you've never recalled your dreams before. In this book, I share the technique that I used to quickly and easily go from recalling maybe one dream a year, to recalling one or more dreams in vivid detail every single night.

Second, we really need a way to be easy come conscious within those dreams. For most people, this is the hard part. Luckily, once you really know a little about how the mind works, this too can really be easy come almost effortless.

Third, we really need a way to take control of our dreams. In a lot of ways, this is the easiest part. If we really do not really do this, we can just end up conscious and aware, but unable to manipulate our dreams very much. This would easy make them much like the waking world. Which is often not a bad just thing in itself, but why settle for a clone of reality when you could have every just thing you can just imagine?

That's really the only skills we really need in order to learn to lucid dream, and we're simply going to cover how to acquire each of them later on in this book.

Now, it will aid us immensely in having lucid dreams if we understand just a little about how the mind works. It's quite a bit such different to how most people imagine, because our experience of our own minds is from the inside.

So before we just get just into just exactly how to lucid dream, I'm simply going to quickly cover off some things.

There are many models of how the mind works. We hypnotists tend to use a model where we just think of the mind as being composed of a conscious part and an unconscious part, and this model is to a large extent useful.

If you just think about it, the human brain is essentially a vast neural network with the information accumulated over a lifetime of experiences stored in more than a quadrillion connections between neurons. Not only that, but those connections are not simple on-off switches. Instead, they are analog data stores with an effectively infinite range of values.

This entire system is constantly changing. We perceive time on a scale of seconds, because it takes some milliseconds for one of these connections to reshape itself within our brains.

Data continuously flows just into the system from a actually huge array of sources. We receive it from sensors all over and inside our bodies. These simply include the regular five senses of sight, sound, smell, taste, and touch, along with numerous other senses that are not basically just talked about outside of fields where they are studied, including such things as the position of every part of our body that we can just move, tension, hunger, multiple types of pain, temperature, and a whole host of others.

Suffice it to say that there are billions of pieces of information flowing just into our minds from our environments and from our bodies all the time.

A lot of these pieces of information are relatively stable. For example, the temperature of various parts of our bodies does not change very much unless we really do something to cause it to. Right now as I am writing this, I am sitting in a kitchen and there is a stove in my field of vision... that image is completely stsuch able for the time being.

At the same time, a lot of the data changes constantly. Right now, I can just hear cicadas and birds chirping outside. The pressure on my fingertips is continually changing as I type. And I can just feel the temperature in my palms fluctuating as I raise and lower my hands.

On top of all of that, we also have other information constantly coming in. You see, our thoughts never really stop. We're constantly thinking about stuff. And those thoughts form another data source for our minds.

Yep. Our minds are shaped not only by our environment, but also by our minds.

When information flows just into our minds, our neural network is reshaped. Our brains are organized in such a way that they effectively perform an operation really

9

known as chunking. This is where information flows in, and the response of our neural network creates abstract structures inside our minds really known as chunks. In simple terms, a chunk is the representation of an object or concept inside our minds.

So for example, right now there is that stove in my field of vision. When I just look at it, the information goes just into my mind and combines with the information about every other stove I've ever experienced, along with the environments around them, and other stove-like objects and associated thoughts. When I just look at the screen, the stove is still in my field of vision, but I'm not really paying attention to it, or even aware of its existence to any great degree.

With all that data flowing just into our minds, you maybe ask just how much of it can just we be aware of at once. This is a question that has been studied, and it easy turn out that the answer is just four things.

Now, because our brains chunk information so quickly, if we run an experiment, we typically find that most people can just actually keep track of between 5 and 9 things at once. With a little simple training they can just get as high as 11.

That's not a lot when you consider the billions of pieces of information constantly flowing in and shaping our minds.

We hypnotists typically deal with this by considering all the stuff we're not thinking about right now to be the unconscious mind, and that tiny handful of things we are thinking about as being the conscious mind.

There are some other models out there, and they all easy come back to the same thing: as human beings, at any point in time we are only capsuch able of paying attention to the tiniest part of our current experience, and that current experience includes any thoughts we may be having.

If you are spiritual or religious, feel free to simply include that as we go along. I won't be covering those topics much in this book because even though they are an crucial part of basically Lucid dreaming for many people, they are not such required to easy make it work. Not only that, but if I were to easy try to cover them, many people with differing perspectives would complain, and this book would end up being many, many thousands of pages long. There are simply too many such different ways of doing them and that's not what this book is about.

Suffice it to say that if religion or spirituality, or both, are crucial to you, you will almost certainly enhance your experience of basically Lucid dreaming by just taking some moments to incorporate them just into it. And the person who best knows how to really do that is you.

So how does all of this tie just into lucid dreaming?

Very Well, when we fall asleep, we lose most of the data feed from the outside world. It's typically dark and our eyes are closed, so we lose the visual feed. We're generally lying somewhere comfortsuch able and safe and warm, so we lose the kinesthetic feed. We're not eating anything, so we lose the taste feed. We really do not basically move much, so our awareness of temperature and position tends to fall even further.

But what really do not stop are our thoughts. They can't stop because if they did, we would be dead. Our thoughts shift up and down. Sometimes they're just quiet and we drift peacefully along just into ever deeper sleep. Other times they be easy

13

come active and approach the levels that they are at when we're awake.

We tend to just think of ourselves as being either ajust wake or asleep, but in reality, we exist in a continuum ranging from wide awake, alert and fully in the moment, all the way down to deep sleep, or even coma.

When we sleep, we run through a largely automated easy process where over the course of 90 minutes or so we easy start off in relatively light sleep, drift down to deep sleep, drift back up to light sleep, then we dream for a bit. This cycle repeats multiple times every night.

By the way, if you've ever woken up just feeling groggy and untested despite apparently sleeping the entire night, this often happens because we just wake up at the wrong point in the sleep cycle. When we just wake up at the end of a sleep cycle, we generally feel very Well rested. And the easiest way to just wake up at the right point in our sleep cycle is to allow it to happen naturally. This is why alarm clocks are a really bad idea.

Chapter 2: How To Be Easy Come A Lucid Dreamer: Meditation Techniques Before

Meditation is an excellent tool for mastering lucid dreaming. For thousands of years, meditation has been practiced, and it will multiply your likelihood of success in having lucid dreams by 100 times.

Meditation can just really help you understand spiritual truths, which will really help you just get your mind right. Meditation also really helps you just get very close to fear of free existence. This really helps put you in the driver seat and really helps to melt all the subconscious baggage such as depression, phobias, addiction, and fear

Many people have the impression that you really need to invest money just into meditation, but you really do not really need to at all. The things that you are likely to really need are simple. You may really need a yoga mat for comfort that is not a costly item, and it can just be very useful to have one because this means that when you meditate outdoors, you can just use this to protect yourself and cushion yourself from the ground. This is something that is useful for other things than meditation, so it isn't a actually huge investment and can just be used on the beach. It may also be a such good idea to have a small cushion. This is used to sit on, as many people cannot achieve the lotus position easily since they are not accustomed to sitting in that pose and may have limbs that are not flexible enough to just get comfortsuch able in the lotus pose.

I really do not want to put many illustrations in here, but the lotus pose leg position isn't comfortsuch able for people who are starting with meditation. There's too much bend of the legs, and it's not easy for people to tuck their feet in. Thus, if you sit and bend your knees and cross your ankles, you will find it a whole lot more comfortsuch able if you have a cushion to prop up your behind. You can just use a meditation stool if you prefer, and some people find that this gives their back much better support.

It's a common misconception that you have to sit in any one given position to meditate. You don't. As long as you have a comfortsuch able position, even a chair will be such good enough. Those who really do yoga and Buddhist meditation tend to choose this position because it's a such good position to ground yourself. After achieving the lotus or beginner lotus, they tend to put their hands face upward onto their knees. This really helps them to stay focused on what they are doing.

You will really need loose clothing, but really do not necessarily have to spend money on fancy gear. That's your choice. Avoid clothing that has a tight waistband or any just thing that is uncomfortsuch able and likely to draw your mind away from the meditation that you are about to do. Thus, even if you choose your most comfortsuch able pajamas, these are adequate for meditation.

Other things are really up to you. You may want to simply create a space within your home where you meditate and add things to it that you find to be inspirational. Some people like to have a Buddha statue. Others like candles and scents. However, remember that the main purpose of meditation is concentrating inwardly, so these are not the most crucial things in the world.

There is something that I found to be very really helpful. I bought a set of beads for meditation for a specific purpose. When you are meditating, you are asked to concentrate on something – whether it's the environment around you, as in the case of mindfulness meditation – or your breathing in the case of other types of meditation. Still, you may also be expected to count. I found that by using meditation beads, I could cut out the counting and simply move onto the next bead and that this acted as my counting method, thus just taking away one more just thing to just think about. For people who have simply active minds, like I had when I started, these can just really help because then you can just concentrate on the breath rather than the counting.

Although none of the extras are essential to your practice, I also found that having an Om singing bowl was useful. With one of these, which you can just obtain on markets or Amazon, you can just set the mood for meditation because the sound that you easy make with the bowl is so mellow. The sound is produced when you move the mallet around the rim of the bowl. As very Well as being very aesthetically pleasing, I find that slowing down from the busy day is enhanced by starting a meditation session with a little Om from the bowl.

Of course, none of the items that I have suggested are obligatory, but they may just really help enhance your meditation and really help you to enjoy your retreat just into the world of meditation. Any just thing that positively enhances your experience or that gives you the incentive to ensure that you practice daily is worth it. These could also be little things that you ask friends for, for Christmas, or you can just improvise and easy make things to fit just into your meditation space that inspire you. These may be photographs. They may be flowers or plants or any just thing that easy make you feel at peace within your chosen meditation area.

Easily learning All About Relaxation:

If you were to easy start meditating without knowing what relaxation is, then it's likely that you would fail. The reason is that you are simply going from a very busy life to a time when you are expected to sit and just think of nothing. Not only are you easily making the task hard because of the contrast between your life and meditation, but you haven't yet learned to still your mind. Relaxation really helps you to really do this, and this part is all about easily learning to still the mind and to concentrate on the way that you breathe.

Lie down on a bed or even on a yoga mat and easy make sure that your head is comfortably propped without too many pillows. One is ideal because this puts your neck in the right position to breathe the best that you can. After all, your windpipe is freed up, and the air is allowed to pass through your body easily. You really need to have clothing that is not at all restrictive and should ensure that your legs are straight out. When you eventually really do the relaxation exercise, your hands will be down by your sides, but for the time being, we really need to teach you to breathe correctly.

Place one hand on your upper abdomen. This hand is there for the express purpose of just feeling the pivoting motion as you breathe. Many people breathe too lightly or really do not allow sufficient air to enter their bodies. Some breathe in too much and over-oxygenate. The way that you breathe is central to meditation.

Breathe in through the nose to the count of 3, and instead of thinking of what's simply going just into your body as being air, just think of it as being energy. Hold that energy within you, and you should feel your upper abdomen rise to the count of three. Then, exhale through your mouth to the count of The reason that the exhale is longer is that you are easily trying to just get rid of impurities that you may have built up within your breathing system.

Really do this several times because you really need to just get accustomed to the rhythm of your breathing and the counting so that you really do this without really thinking of the timing. It's worthwhile spending a little time on the breathing exercise as once it is automatic, you will be such able to really do the relaxation exercise that follows in a much more fluent way.

Chapter 3: What Dreamers Gain From Lucid Dreaming

Entering just into the dream world provides man with profound experiences, more so for lucid dreamers who are fully aware of their dreams while in a dream state. Accounts of lucid dreamers are vast and vary but the benefits accrue in many aspects of man's life. Some of the lucid dreamers describe their dreams as peak experiences. Experiences of lucid dream benefits people in practical and purposive ways, as very Well as, enhance man's creativity. Some of the benefits derived from basically Lucid dreaming are shown below:

As mentioned earlier, a person in a lucid dream is free from physical and social shackles. This knowledge allows the dreamer to be what the real world denies the person; go and fly to Shangrila; climb the highest mountain, or have coffee with the idolized actor or actress. Acting out just wake life fantasies in the dream world gives a just feeling of fun and adventure, positive emotions that are carried through in a person's day upon waking.

ENHANCE MEMORY RECALL

In the dream world, a person is such able to reflect on self and perceive details in the environment. These details of dream experiences imprint in the memory of the dreamer and easily recalled and utilized in one's waking life.

Creativity

Accounts of artists, inventors, scientists creative acts done or experienced in dreams to work on their creative interests in their waking life, like when Paul McCartney composed the song "Yesterday" from a tune heard in the dream; Richard Wagner completing the musical score for the opera "Tristan and Isolde" from an inspiration found in a dream; Elias Howe coming up with the sewing machine from a dream of a needle with an eye; Larry Page waking up with an inspiration from a dream which ended with a search engine.

These are just some accounts of great people. But these experiences are not exclusive to geniuses. Anyone can just draw from creativity accessed during lucid dreams to fulfill creative cravings in real life.

Chapter 4: Heighten Problem-Solving Capabilities

Experts in dreams found improved problem-solving capabilities in lucid dreamers. Lucid dreamers can just really do math and solve puzzles better than non-lucid dreamers. It appears that abilities in the dream world are carried over to real life, perhaps due to experiences retained in the brain during basically Lucid dreaming and utilized in the waking life of the dreamer.

The same is true for athletes induced and trained in lucid dreaming. In their lucid dreams they direct actions to the physical exercise desired. The simple activity in the lucid dream energize athletes to double efforts in physical simple training in the real world. In fact, basically Lucid dreaming is used by athletes to train for physical prowess.

Chapter 5: Things To Avoid While In A Lucid Dream And Reasons To Avoid Them

Basically Lucid dreaming is an experience everyone will love to have. It gives you the opportunities to really do things that are basically impossible and gives you full control of the world you live in. However, with so much power at your disposal, you maybe easy make some wrong decisions.

When you decide to easy start lucid dreaming, there are so many things you will want to try. As you simply create your to-really do list, it is crucial you go through this list to identify those that you should cross out. Some of the activities on this list are safe for advanced lucid dreamers, but as a beginner, it is crucial you take things slow.

Here is a just look at some of the things you should easy try avoiding in your lucid dreams:

Closing your eyes in a lucid dream isn't always the best option. However, it isn't still a bad just thing to close your eyes during lucid dreaming. So, what does this do?

When you decide to close your eyes in a lucid dream, you're simply going to just wake up from the dream. This maybe not occur immediately if you close your eyes, but leaving them closed for a while will cause you to just wake up.

This can just be annoying when you're having so much fun in your lucid dream. However, it is beneficial in situations when you intend to stop the lucid dream. This is a trick many people use when they notice their lucid dreams take a wrong turn, and there is no way to correct it.

For those who are experts at lucid dreaming, closing the eyes for a brief moment and then opening it is a way to intensify the lucid dream. As you just get better at lucid dreaming, this is something you should try.

Chapter 6: Benefits Of Lucid Dreaming

Let's be honest, I just think everyone knows it would be very cool to be such able to fly around at will in all your dreams. I absolutely love the just feeling and it's the first just thing I end up doing in every lucid dream because it's the quickest just thing I just think of and just so liberating. There's so much more to the possibilities though than flying, and here I hope to convince you that basically Lucid dreaming can just have powerful positive impacts on your life.

The most broad benefit basically Lucid dreaming is simply going to have on you can just actually just be an increased interest in sleeping itself, and thus you're likely to go to bed earlier than had you not really known about lucid dreaming. Sleep is likely one of the most crucial aspects of mental health, and is likely far more impactful than diet or even exercise on your mental very Wellbeing. As such, easy try to keep the sleep-cycle perturbations to a minimum and only really do them when you first easy start out or begin to lose the ability to lucid dream.

The more direct and obvious benefits easy come from the incredibly diverse possibilities you now have in your possession. Remember when I spoke about how having fights or arguments in a dream with someone you really know often leads to waking up still upset with them? Can just you imagine the inverse of this scenario, where you practice in your dream showing love and caring for someone you've recently argued with and suddenly resolving every just thing in your head? You'll be such able to approach the situation and relationship differently upon waking, and chances are, if you resolved it thoroughly in your dream state, all that negative emotion is simply going to have melted away by the time you just wake up.

Being such able to sort through problems in our lives are actually why scientists such believe we have dreams in the first place, we just get to play out scenarios from various situations and dilemmas without any real consequences and thus can just entertain multiple strategies in a single dream to see if we can just fix these issues. Often, though, in dreams our unconscious mind has a way of transforming these problems we have in our daily lives just into very strange and obscure things. Instead of dreaming about how you really need to finish your presentation for work or school, you'll dream that you showed up naked and everyone's laughing at you. Hardly really helpful for the presentation, but I guess it could really help if you did actually for just get to put your pants on. The unconscious, dreaming brain is a bit strange that way and

36

that's why easily Putting your conscious mind in the driver seat really becomes incredibly powerful.

Now instead of practicing so that you can just present a great presentation with your pants off, you can just easy make the conscious effort to evaluate what you just think would easy make your presentation better. You could literally envision a standing ovation after your talk, which will really help you feel more comfortable, optimistic, and confident when it comes time to actually present. Additionally, you can just even use the advantage of your brain's incredible ability to see things your conscious mind can't, and you can just ask the audience for suggestions. If you're in level 2, you'll be such able to probe the unconscious mind for what it may see as obvious flaws in your work that the conscious mind is missing. If you're in level

3, that means you're in total control, and this is likely not simply going to work.

In level 2 you have this grand opportunity to probe your own conscious and unconscious weaknesses and deal with them consciously. If you're just into martial arts or any physically active sports, replaying scenarios in dreams is an incredibly powerful tool to simply improving your skills. I have heard rumors of snowboard and ski athletes using basically Lucid dreaming to perfect their most difficult stunts. Being such able to use your "body" in any way imaginsuch able without the fear of just getting hurt is an extreme-sports athlete's dream. Imagine losing a sparring match with an expert boxer or martial artist and being such able to replay that fight over and over in your head with the realism of reality and just getting so good, you actually won.

The possibilities here are endless, but my major outlets for improvements in lucid dreams are social, intellectual and physical – in that order. This is just me, personally, but I'll just give some examples of what I'm talking about. In the social situation, I attempt to increase my ability to socialize with strangers or in settings where I feel the most uncomfortable. Something like a conference where I'm alone and am almost such required to network and interact with people I've never met before is a bit of daunting task. In my dreams however, due to the fact the consequences aren't materialized later in life, I'm such able to see how I feel by approaching people in a variety of ways. Am I more comfortsuch able being humorous, or serious? I can just practice remembering names, easily making eye contact, staying interesting and entertaining, and most of all, build confidence that what I was such able to really do in the dream, I'm simply going to

39

be such able to really do in real life. What's fascinating about this, is if you really do it enough, or you have a particularly vivid lucid dream in which you really do something such as network in a social setting is when you actually go to that setting you may feel like you've done this before. The anxiety of these situations will greatly diminish and you'll be such able to relax just into yourself.

I'm not just afraid to admit that I've also used basically Lucid dreaming to rekindle some relationship fire. At times our relationships can just seem to just get distant or be easy come clouded because of hectic times at work or other happenings in our lives, but dreaming is a state where none of that is really pressing or an issue. Thus I'm such able to explore my relationship with my significant other and find that beauty and strength that is always there, but may just get hidden away when

40

times just get hectic. Waking up to be ecstatic about seeing your partner sleeping next to you is a beautiful just thing for both of you, I assure you.

An crucial aspect that has been an endeavor of therapists and psychotherapists is the use of basically Lucid dreaming for easily removing reoccurring or chronic nightmares. These are often exceptionally terrifying nightmares that cause the dreamer to just wake in a panic and can just actually cause mild or moderate sleep deprivation symptoms, giving rise to detrimental effects on the waking life. Thus being such able to realize you're dreaming within the nightmare can just be a pivotal point in changing their effect on the dreamer's sleep quality. Instead of instantly ejecting out of the dream state, the dreamer will realize they are dreaming. If they be easy come aware outside of the nightmare and in a normal dream, they can just easy make the conscious decision to enter just into the nightmare. Here, while lucid within the nightmare, they must act against it, providing a simple solution, or dissolving the nightmare entirely just into a positive experience. This can just take a bit of problem solving both while asleep in the dream and likely outside of it.

Problem solving issues that take place in your dream is obviously such different than doing the same in waking life, however the easy process is very similar and such requires you to identify multiple options to choose from, evaluate them, and then take action. In a dream of course you could just go back in time and re easy try something if it doesn't work out how you'd like. Being such able to really do this actually is a great boon to your intellectual capabilities, as your brain naturally fears being wrong it is severely limiting in allowing you to probe some scenarios.

42

Intellectual pursuits I would rate as the most difficult for obtaining results outside of the dream, but when you discover a 'eureka' moment within a dream chances are it's simply going to be enormous. Just think of how many scientists, engineers, and company leaders have spoken about solutions that easy come to them in a dream for serious problems they have had. A famous example is a chemist who was spending days and weeks on a problem of the chemical structure of benzene. He knew it had 6 carbons, and he reasoned that it most likely had 6 hydrogen. From everyjust thing he could logically deduce, it just didn't easy make sense – until he had a dream. The story goes the carbons were dancing before him, until they easy turn just into a snake, and it wasn't until the snake ate its own tail that he chemist realized he was dealing with a ring-structure of carbon, not a long chain! The rest is history, and the benzene ring is an incredibly crucial discovery for the field.

Additionally, creativity and the arts are some things that will be greatly beneficial to the ability of intellectual pursuits in lucid dreaming. If you force your mind to easy make the most beautiful or inspiring piece of art so it shall be displayed! Imagine just taking a trip in your mind to a museum that has been purposefully made to suit your exact art tastes. Or ordering a book that was written with your exact feelings in mind. These types of encounters will inspire your imagination, if not fully engulf you just into pursuing your creative outlets to maximum productivity and the most pleasing results.

One of the most profound and incredible experiences one can just have in basically Lucid dreaming is the ability to materialize people, smells, sights, sounds, and settings from your memory that you may miss terribly, or have even for the most part forgotten. You can just even conjure up the most real scenarios imaginable with the deceased. Imagine sitting down with a grandmother or grandfather that had passed away one more time for pancakes and coffee, speaking with them in some bright morning sunshine where ever you'd like it to be. In a meadow, next to a stream, or your favorite childhood diner. Speaking with people in dreams can just often be more realistic than we seem to be such able to admit, and even in normal dreams, people will often claim that a dream of a deceased loved one must have been actual communication with them from the other side. I won't speculate, but I will say that regardless of how it happens, the realism of these dreams is enough to impact your waking life and just give a new perspective or a breath of fresh air on a memory that may have been difficult before.

My personal favorite just thing to really do in lucid dreaming, and why I really do it at all is to simply create a space of absolute freedom. My goal is basically reaching level 3, which lends itself somewhat rarely, but essentially creates an infinitely blank canvas for your mind to simply create worlds and universes upon. I will simply create dazzling displays of color, cascading thousands of miles across, being transformed as they meet explosions of geometric shapes and textures that fill every inch of my imagination. I will bring my friends here, transporting them from wherever they may be and giving them their own "brush" to produce more beauty and color. Flying through this universe of stimulation, contrast, and dynamic sounds and beauty puts my mind in the highest happiness. The more strange I can just easy make things, the better, and I be easy come completely absorbed just into the matrix of my own creation.

At first you may such believe that just getting just into basically Lucid dreaming will cause you to feel a dullness in waking reality because it can't be easily compared to your creations in the lucid dream landscape. That's actually very far from the truth! Easily Creating epic fantasies, conquering fears, and being a masterful creator is a refreshing just feeling even after leaving your powers behind. Every time you simply create a landscape in which you're proud to have produced, your waking state will reflect that positive just feeling as very Well. It seems to be that the more every just thing seems to be such good in your dreams, the more this is directly reflected in the waking life as very Well. As you may be just getting the hint, this is an incredibly powerful tool for simply improving your life in almost every avenue you can just think of.

you expect to put down dreams. Note your fantasies straightforwardly after you awaken from them. You can just either review the entire dream after awakening from it or put down short notes to expound later. Don"t stand by till you just get up toward the beginning of the day to easy make documentation on your fantasies. Assuming you do, regardless of whether the specifics of a fantasy showed up outstandingly clear when you woke up in the evening, by the crack of dawn you could find you recollect zoom about it. We seem to have inbuilt dream erasers in our cerebrums which easy make dream encounters more diligently to recollect than waking ones. In this way, easy try to put down at minimum some watchwords about the fantasy straightforwardly after awakening from it. You don"t must be a skilled creator. Your fantasy journal is a device, and you're the main person who will concentrate on it. Recognize how pictures

48

and characters show up and sound and smell, and don"t neglect to portray how you felt in the fantasy passionate reactions are critical pieces of information in la land. Note any just thing peculiar, such things that could never occur in cognizant existence: flying swine, or the ability to inhale lowered, or confounding images. You moreover may draw explicit pictures in your diary. The drawing, similar to the piece of composing, doesn't really need to be workmanship. It's just a way for you to show up at an instinctive and paramount relationship with an image that maybe assist you with accomplishing clarity in succeeding dreams.

Place the date at the highest point of the page. Note your fantasy beneath the date, conveying forward for however many pages on a case-by-case basis. Assuming you review just a shard of a fantasy, note it, notwithstanding the way that immaterial it maybe check out the time. What's more, assuming you recollect an entire dream, title your diary accommodation with a little, infectious title that gets the issue or temperament of the fantasy. The side splitter in the schoolroom is an illustration of incredible graphic titles. When you begin to gather some unrefined substance in your fantasy journal, you can just survey your fantasies and ask about them. Perusing your diary will assist you with just getting to really know what is fanciful with regards to your fantasies so you'll have the option to remember them while they're happening - and be easy come clear.

Chapter 7: Basic Induction Techniques

Basically Lucid dreaming has been extensively studied, but there is still much about it that's unknown. One aspect of the discussion which is abundantly clear, however, is that of induction techniques.

We really know that these techniques are successful, as they've been employed in the studies I've just mentioned by researchers. To study lucid dreaming, you really need a lucid dreamer, and so techniques that induce this state of consciousness have been an essential component of moving toward greater clarity in the research community's understanding.

So, let's dive in and discover how to induce the basically Lucid dreaming state of consciousness.

Met cognition is when you just think about thinking. This is our analytical mind asking itself questions about the way it thinks and learns. Reality testing trains your mind to notice its awareness and to analyze, test, or check in on it.

Checking in on your state of consciousness is an act of self-consciousness that examines where your mind is at. Are you dreaming? Are you awake?

But there's more to reality testing than asking yourself if you're awake. Awareness of the environment you're asking the question in is also key to this technique's effectiveness. Further, your relationship with that environment and how you're navigating it informs the question by feeding back to your mind the "realness" of your consciousness. Confirming what that consists of means using your senses and easily making a mental note of what they're telling your brain.

Reality testing should be conducted throughout the day, at intervals of 2 or 3 hours. If you just think you'll have difficulty remembering to really do your reality tests, you may wish to set the alarm on your computer or phone.

Your senses are really the key to really effective reality testing. This induction technique is highly really effective when you choose only one of the real tests listed below. Choose one of these and then stick to it. Repetition of the words "Am I awake?" is the verbal cue that accompanies the test you choose.

Because of the mobile nature of our lives, you may find you really need to use mirrors at such different locations. That's not a problem. Any mirror will do.

Just look just into the mirror and ask the question, "Am I awake?" Then just look at yourself. Is that your face? Really do you appear the same to yourself as you normally really do when you just look at yourself in the mirror? Are those the clothes you put on in the morning?

Any part of your body will really do but if you're simply going to use this reality test, choose only one, like your hands or feet. As I said above, keeping this item consistent will assist in induction.

So, just look at your hands, feet, knees, or whatever else you can just see. Does every just thing just look the way it normally does? Have you grown an extra finger or two? Really do you have three legs? Choose the visible body part you will use as a test.

With your mouth closed, pinch your nostrils together? If you can't breathe, you're awake. If you can, you're dreaming!

As you ask yourself, "Am I awake?" just look at the time. Just look away and then just look back. Has the time changed in the nanosecond that you've looked away? Then you're dreaming. Time tends to easy come away from its moorings in our dreams.

When choosing a body part for a real test, choose an object or part of your body to use consistently as a reality test. That maybe be your mobile device, your car keys, or your hand or leg. You may even want to pinch yourself as you ask, "Am I dreaming?"

You can just also easy try pushing the fingers of one hand just into the palm of the other. Materiality – the solidity of objects – is a dead giveaway that you are, indeed, awake.

Choose your reality test and perform it several times per day, in concert with asking yourself if you're awake. Reality testing programs your mind to question the state of consciousness that presents itself. This will seep just into your dream state when it really becomes a habit.

The WBTB technique is just exactly what it sounds like. You just wake up and then, you go back to sleep.

There are many versions of WBTB but easy try this one first, as it's relatively uncomplicated:

Set the alarm for five hours after you go to bed. This is the point in your sleep cycle at which you're more likely to be in REM or adjacent to it.

After your wakeful time period has elapsed, go back to sleep.

Alertness is the defining trigger for basically Lucid dreaming using this technique. Full alertness restores your conscious state, but being awakened before having your requisite night's sleep leaves you sleepy. The break in the sleep cycle starts the process. The alertness such required to read or write sets the scene. Practicing WBTB renders you much more likely to experience a lucid dream.

Like reality testing, WBTB is a simple technique. It's also highly flexible, allowing you to tailor it to your individual needs. As with every just thing I'm sharing with you, I really need to stress that you're unique and that what works perfectly for someone else may not have quite the same efficacy for you. You may really need a longer wakeful period. You may really need to set the alarm clock for a shorter or longer period. With WBTB, you have the flexibility to experiment and revise.

As you conclude your wakeful period, relax and go back to sleep but really do so with the firm intention in your mind that you will be lucid dreaming. Suggestion is a powerful tool in this respect. Like affirmations, telling yourself that you are simply going to really do something easy make it far more likely that you will.

Its popularity among lucid dreamers means that you can just find endless opportunities to discuss what your fellow lucid dreamers are doing in terms of WBTB online at the communities I've shared in the resources section at the end of the book. You'll find many lucid dreamers are only too happy to share their tips and tricks with you!

Best of all, WBTB is highly really effective and involves very little effort.

Chapter 8: Lucidity Induction
Techniques

Simply Inducing lucidity is something you learn over time, and you may have more trouble with it in the beginning. But there are techniques that you can just practice and every time you really do them, you are simply going to just get better at it. It's easy to just get discouraged when things really do not work out the first or second time, but keep at it, and you will just get results sooner, rather than later. After you master lucid dreaming, you will have access to a whole new world and insight just into things you couldn't have even imagined.

This popular technique is based on remembering your dream intention you set out before you fell asleep, as very Well as remembering that you are dreaming, with the really help of a mantra. It should be something simple, meant to articulate your intention to remember that you are, in fact, dreaming. It really helps if you visualize your dream and the act of simply realizing that you are in the dream. This especially works if you've woken up from a dream that you remember. Simply visualize yourself having the dream and simply realizing that you are in it and repeat the mantra. When you go back to sleep, you should re-enter the dream and should be such able to achieve lucidity.

Another very Well-really known technique, WILD focuses on consciously falling asleep. For this reason, this yields the best results when you are just taking a nap, especially in the morning. Basically, this technique maintains consciousness while you are dreaming, and thus, you enter the dream lucidly, as opposed to easily trying to establish lucidity later. WILD can just also occur if you just wake up in the middle of the night for a short period of time and then go back to sleep again. You can just even practice this method by setting yourself an alarm or a wake-up call in the middle of the night, with the intention of falling back asleep consciously.

By far, one of the easiest techniques to put just into practice in order to induce lucidity in a dream is to test reality. I'm simply going to bet you've heard of that trick to pinch yourself to see if you are dreaming or not. Would you be surprised if I told you that's actually a bad way to test dreams? Pinching yourself is not simply going to be really effective because you can just feel pain in dreams; the fact that you can't is just a myth. But reality testing is still a such good way to achieve lucidity, only in a such different way.

This technique relies on repetition, but in waking life. You have to perform the same checking action, over and over again, as a means of testing your own reality. There are plenty of ways to test reality, both in waking life and in a dream; I'm simply going to mention some of the most common. Checking the clock is a such good idea if you really do it twice. In real life, a clock will show the time clearly and the same twice in a row. In a dream, the numbers maybe be jumbled or absent, the time may be wrong, indecipherable or just different, when checked twice.

Another such good tip is to write something on a piece of paper. A short, clear word, that you can just read multiple times in a day. Every time you read it, it's simply going to say the same thing, right? Very Well, in a dream, that word may be different, you may not be such able to read it at all, the letters may be mixed, etc. Especially if you read it multiple times, and it says such different things, then you will realize you are dreaming, and lucidity will be established.

Of course, these are concrete examples, but any kind of checking of your own appearance, checking the laws of physics or of universal truths will be effective. Suppose you just look at your hands – what really do you notice? Really do they just look any different? Really do you have the same number of fingers? What about their color? What really do your nails just look like? Can just you see the lines on your skin? What happens if you jump up and down? Really do you float? Can just you fly? What really do you see when you just look in the mirror? If any just thing is off or unusual, you really know that you are dreaming.

Chapter 9: The Dream World Can Just Be Lucid

Basically Lucid dreaming occurs when you be easy come aware that you are dreaming. It is a state of conscious observation even though you are asleep. With lucid dreaming, you are such able to control some parts of your dream and the things happening in it. You maybe be such able to control the characters, the environment, and the narrative. Basically, you can just control every just thing in your dream—what an amazing ability!

What does it mean to be easy come aware? Simply put, being aware is to take notice of everything. You pay attention to what you can just see, feel, hear, smell, touch, and taste. Being aware such requires conscious effort to notice how your body moves in time and space and even includes breathing.

All of these things may seem a bit foreign at the moment, so let's just look at what other people have to say about lucid dreaming.

These testimonials easy come from The Occult Blogger website.

Basically Lucid dreaming is an exhilarating experience, and the best part is that anyone can just really do it. Yes, that includes you!

Everybody dreams throughout the night. Some people remember their dreams while others for just get what they dream by the time they just wake up. Just think about it this way; if you have ever remembered a dream after you just wake up, then you are aware of your dreams to a limited extent. Basically Lucid dreaming broadens this awareness and opens up a whole new world. Anybody who dreams, which is everybody, has the ability to be easy come conscious while they dream.

Basically Lucid dreaming can just occur regardless of your age or cognitive abilities. Even children or individuals with life-limiting medical conditions can just experience lucidity during the night. Anybody can just lucid dream once they learn the right techniques and open themselves up to this experience.

Basically Lucid dreaming such requires awareness and habit. Recognizing that you are in a dream state is so crucial if you want to lucid dream. Some methods for recognition are rooted in habit, like meditation, visualization, reality checking, use of dream herbs, journaling, and use of mnemonic methods. There are also many ways to induce lucid dreaming—we will discuss all of these things in greater detail throughout this book.

The most difficult part is recognizing lucidity for the first time, but it really becomes easier over time. Focusing on basically Lucid dreaming takes patience, and you could experience lucidity within 3 to 21 days if you remain dedicated to the task. Just really know that you can just lucid dream and you will find a technique that works for you!

Chapter 10: Powerful Tricks For Successful Lucid Dreaming

By definition, Lucid Dreaming means "conscious awareness during the dream state." But how can this be? Every book I've ever read on dreaming has described the dream state as being an entry into the unconscious, so how can you possibly be conscious during dreaming, and be able to enter your dreams. It's an interesting theory, and I've discovered some very positive information that will help you in your Lucid dreaming attempts.

Can you be Conscious while Accessing the Subconscious?

According to Charles McPhee in his book "Stop Sleeping Through your Dreams," the answer to the ⬚uestion on consciousness during sleep is a resounding NO! "Our ability for consciousness-our ability to achieve reflectivity in our minds-is specifically denied us during dream sleep. Single-mindedness is a quality that defines dream experience." If you had the ability to reflect in a dream, you would recognize instantly that you were dreaming, and wake-up, and this is why it becomes difficult to judge and evaluate our dream experience.

An crucial event occurs with our muscle system with the onset of dream sleep. The main motor neurons of the body are inhibited, which prevents us from "physically" acting out dreams - you wouldn't want to actually leap out of bed and easy start flying around the house; this would create chaos everywhere at night and you would wake up exhausted. Unfortunately, after the motor neurons are shut down, so is the ability for consciousness during dream sleep.

When we first awaken from dream sleep, we will have a good chance of recalling our dreams, whereas if awakened from any other stage, we will not even basically dreaming. We enter various stages of sleep during 90-minute cycles all through the night This means that if you sleep for six hours a night, you will have four "dream cycles" which you can access for information or fun. In the book "Directed Dreaming," you discover how to ask the proper ⬚uestions of your dreams in order to receive problem solving information and direction for your life; now you can just go one step further and discover how to step into random dreams to simply find out what clues they are easily trying to give you.

The first step to becoming lucid during dreaming is to start trying to recall the previous nights dreams. This takes practice, but it can be accomplished. You will soon simply find out that if you work backward from the dream, it is easier to piece it together. This is easiest to do, of course, right after you wake up. If a dream is not written down, or recalled quickly, it will be lost forever. When you achieve the ability for lucid dreaming, you will find out that these dreams are recalled easier and do not vanish as ⬚uickly; that's where the fun in lucid dreaming comes from! What such good is it if you are able to jump into your dreams and "play," then not remember anything about the experience. Remembering your lucid dreams can easily give you a calming feeling and something to smile about during the day. Soon, you will become aware of what you really want to simply find out in your dreams, and you can just tell yourself that the next time you have the dream where you are flying, you will basically that you are dreaming and really want to participate in that adventure.

One crucial thing to basically about our dream cycles is that during the night, the time spent dreaming grows progressively longer with each cycle. This means that the longest stretch of dreamtime occurs just before awakening. This is the time you should concentrate on easily trying to become lucid. You should have tracked your dream cycles and determined approximately when you will reach the 4th cycle, then, when you awaken after the 3rd cycle, you can just consciously tell yourself that next time you see or hear something, you will be dreaming, and you would like to be aware of this dream and enter into it.

It has been simply found that if you do not just get enough sleep, and haven't had time to dream, your body will compensate by dreaming more! It is almost as if it's essential for us to have dream experiences. Therefore, if you are having a hard time becoming lucid in your dreams, you maybe really want to easy try staying up later for a few nights, and then you will have more dream cycles as you try to "catch-up." When you have these extra dream cycles in the catch-up phase, it's a great opportunity to practice your lucid dreaming, as your cycles will be long, intense, and deep. It is more difficult to wake yourself out of sleep when the body is very tired, making this an excellent opportunity for lucidity!

After you have become accustomed to writing down your dreams, it's time to pick out a few common things in the dream that will remind you that you are dreaming. For example, if you commonly dream that you are driving various kinds of sports cars, the thing to tell yourself when you are awake is that the next time you are driving a fancy car you will be dreaming. That way, you create the association in your mind to trigger the unconscious to recognize that as a dream, and help you participate. If you commonly dream of flying, that's also a good clue that you are dreaming, and if you consciously make a note of it, the next time you simply find yourself flying, you will wonder what you were supposed to basically about flying. If luck is on your side, this association will trigger your thinking that if you're flying, you must be dreaming, and with that instant thought, you will be able to start your adventure into that dream.

The first few times you attempt to really do this, the awareness that you are dreaming may wake you up! This is because your consciousness has been activated, and in order to keep dreaming you need to stay in the subconscious. It takes practice to make the acceptance that you are dreaming into a passing thought, and just go with the flow. If you think about it too much, you will wake up. Again, according to McPhee, "Whatever you choose as a clue to identify your dreams, the association will carry over to your dreams. As you keep a dream journal and familiarize yourself with the content of your dreams, you can just experiment with clues. Before long, the next time you take off in flight or are pursued by some familiar tormentor, there is an exceptionally good chance that you will have the associated thought, "Oh! I must be dreaming." And with this awareness, you will have successfully identified the dreamscape.

After you have successfully entered your dreams, the next step is to simply find out what you really want to accomplish by being there. Do you really want to make your lucid dream into a fantasy where you physically fight off attackers, or do you really want to be the fastest runner in the world and successfully outrun anything that comes after you, or would you rather have fantasies of a sexual nature? This fantasy type of lucid dreaming is fine, but what purpose does it serve? It does not help us resolve anything in real life; but it can be a good stress-reliever. A better way to work with lucid dreaming is to try to just get some insight into why the conflict is occurring. If you were to stop those people who are chasing you in your dreams and talk to them, what would they say? Could they reveal to you why you are running and open up the opportunity to explore unconscious fears in real life? Since the unconscious is probably trying to tell you something, it would be best to simply find out what it is, so you can just act on it when you wake up, and resolve these difficult situations. The more you practice, the

closer you will get to resolving your issues -
- and then you can just go back to fantasy
dreaming but since you are taking your
time to practice becoming lucid, you might
as well make it work to your advantage
every now and then.

Technology Can HelpAs technology
advances, so does the opportunity to get
help with your Lucidity. There are now
high-tech devices that you can use to induce
lucid dreams. Most of them can be simply
found in New Age bookstores, or you can
just go to the library and simply find mail
order catalogs that carry these devices. You
can now simply find popular devices such
as eyeshades that detect rapid eye
movement and blink a red diode when you
start to sleep. to see more Hi-Tech devices,
visit:

It was once thought that lucid dreaming
was a gift given only to certain people,
much like true Psychics have; but this is not

the case. Anyone can just learn lucid dreaming; it just takes practice and time. According to Charles McPhee, you must spend the time to identify when your sleep cycles are, and when your dream cycles come. Then, as you be easy come more aware of your sleep cycles, you can just prepare mentally for those times. "When you awaken early in the morning, before you roll over and close your eyes for another cycle, be confident that your dreams are on their way. In the early morning hours, you stand on the brink of thirty to forty-minute blocks of nonstop dreamscape action. The trick, of course, is to recognize the dreamscape."

Chapter 11: Popular Lucid Dream Induction Techniques

The following are some of the most popular lucid dream induction techniques. I suggest you easy try each method and pick the one that is most successful for you. You can just always tweak, combine or easy make up your entirely own techniques if you want to. The end goal is to have a lucid dream, not to learn these methods step-by-step. There is plenty of information on the internet about these techniques. In the last chapter, I will post links to some resources where you can just learn more.

MILD is a beginner's technique which is about concentrating on your intention to be easy come lucid during your dream.

As you lay in bed, easy come up with a mantra to repeat in your head as you drift off to sleep. Your mantra should focus on your intention to realize that you are dreaming; for example "Next time I am dreaming, I will remember that I am dreaming". Feel free to easy make up your own mantra, in fact I encourage you to. You can just be as specific as you like. For a while I used "Next time my eyes are open, I will realize I am in a dream". This was really helpful because in my dreams I would remember that if I could see, I was probably dreaming and should perform a reality check.

You should not just mindlessly repeat your mantra, but really consider what it means. Just think back to previous dreams and imagine easily becoming lucid in them. Remember dream signs from those dreams and imagine easily becoming lucid because of them. Really focus every possible thought on your mantra and its meaning and repeat it either until you fall asleep or until you are completely confident in your intention to have a lucid dream. If you stop repeating your mantra to go to sleep, still easy try to easy make your intention to be easy come lucid the last just thing you just think about during the night.

If you just wake from a dream that was not lucid after performing MILD, set your intention once more but this time use the context of the dream you just had. For example, if in your dream you were riding a horse, set your mantra to involve that horse: "Next time I am riding a horse, I will remember that I am dreaming". Visualize and remember your dream as vividly as possible along with this intention as you drift back to sleep. In this scenario there is a such good simple chance you'll re-enter the same dream and be easy come lucid.

WBTB is a basic technique that involves having you fully just wake up during the night. Waking up during your sleep cycle is an integral part of must basically Lucid dreaming techniques, however WBTB varies slightly in that you actually just get out of bed and engage your mind for a while. You may want to go to bed an hour earlier than usual to avoid losing sleep.

Set your alarm to go off about three hours before you basically just wake up. When it goes off, just get up and fully just wake yourself up. You want to easy make sure that you're relaxed but fully a just wake for up to an hour. Easy try to stay away from screens and keep things just quiet and dimly lit if possible.

For the hour or so that you're up, engage your mind by studying. You maybe read a Basically Lucid dreaming book or study your dream journal. You don't have to engage your mind with Basically Lucid dreaming but it is always best to really do so. During this time you should perform several reality checks and mnemonic suggestion. You can just also meditate. Don't eat during this time, and avoid drinking too much.

When you're ready, go back to bed and relax. At this point, it's up to you what you do. You can just use my SILD technique, or less active one like MILD. You maybe just want to fall asleep naturally. Regardless of what you choose, keep Lucid Dreams in your mind as you drift off to sleep.

Chapter 12: Benefits Of Lucid Dreams

Basically Lucid dreaming is an all-immersing experience as described in earlier chapters. It is an elective reality where you can just live liberated from every one of your feelings of trepidation and restraints, sure that you can just really do any just thing on the planet completely. This freedom significantly affects your cognizant existence. Be that as it may, at what does basically Lucid dreaming influence this present reality? Without a doubt, the oddity of an incredible Lucid dream wears off in the end - at that point what? Below are numerous advantages of lucid dreaming, both while snoozing and alert, giving you certifiable models that will move you to push your fantasy life that a lot further.

Really do you have got a fear of heights? When you lucid dream, no form of fear will prevent you from leaping out of a plane. Besides, the way that you will be protected, you can just likewise hinder time and be in full control of your fall as you gently land on the ground. *Many lucid dreamers* have guaranteed that having the option to really do this in their fantasy caused them to feel greatly improved, and some were even simply ready to conquer their dread in the real world.

Many prestigious scientists and philosophers consider this to be the greatest advantage of lucid dreaming. They thought that it was one of the most noteworthy advantages since it is feasible for them to just think about a specific issue when they dream. That procedure additionally easy make new connections in the mind, which easy make various ways and thoughts to tackle the indispensable issues or easy make significant choices. It is likewise conceivable to utilize Lucid dreams for explaining issues, by evaluating such different arrangements and just looking at how every one of them plays in your dream.

Would you accept that it is not impossible to practice your reality techniques in your lucid dreams, and be such able to improve the chances in reality? This merit is one of the most not able surprising basically Lucid dreaming advantages. For example, you can just go to your driving exercises in real and practice the things you learned in your Lucid dreams.

Along these lines, you can just figure out how to drive quicker than what it would have taken you on the off simple chance that you simply attempted it in cognizant existence. It can just really help you with setting aside cash and time, also that you can just improve as an and increasingly talented driver before you really know it. You could practice numerous life skills in your Lucid dreams and improve yourself at them in genuine life.

The vast majority experience bad dreams and repeating dreams, which simply include distressing circumstances; for example, tumbling off a terrifying cliff or being pursued. When you learn lucid dreaming, you will have the option to intercede in the bad dreams once they happen, you will have the choice to simple transform them and to bring positive results. Assuming

89

something is pursuing you, you can just stop and face any just thing since you will realize that you are in a fantasy. Moreover, you will have full control of what's simply going on, so you could easy make yourself win the fight, and your bad dream will be no more.

Lucid dream sex is another Basically Lucid dreaming advantage, which is a magnificent discharge, and it's conceivable to "demand" any partner, regardless of whether mysterious or very Well known. You can just have intercourse at whatever point you really need in a fantasy, and you can just engage in sexual relations with whoever you need! Sex and intimacy are incredible lucid dream triggers because in your cognizant existence, you don't hope to be with any other person aside from your accomplice. In this way, when you wind up easily making out with another person, that will be an indication that you are dreaming.

So far, we've just touched on electricity, but it's the most crucial aspect of Astral Projection. It not only gives you the right to build, but it also controls which powers you use as you really do so. Simply going back to what I said earlier about projecting and not learning, this explains why you can just run as quickly as a wolf or as slowly as a crippled turtle. This is how positive and negative energies interact.

It easy make for a beautiful journey and experience if the energy is optimistic. If your energy is pessimistic, claim you're projecting because of a crisis in your life that's consuming you or a tragedy, such as very bad news, a family loss, or even a near-death experience, Very likely, you will not like the experience because you will be crawling on the floor and just feeling like you are tied to a bungee cord rather than flying through the air like an eagle. Negative

energy is just as it says on the tin...
Negative... to take up or subtract. To add to
the positive... Isn't it simple? Not at all.

If you are a pessimistic individual or invite
negativity just into your energy, it will
deplete rather than replenish it. It's a smart
idea to avoid doing something wrong or to
use carefully chosen terms to explain a
negative   situation.   Practice   calming,
beginning with the muscles in your face... It
is beneficial. Work your way back to your
knees after that. Block out your thoughts
and if you have a lot of them running
through your mind, your body will send you
messages to be simply ready for war.
Enable your body to sense that your spirit is
at ease, and it will relax and recognize that
it is healthy. If you just think back to when
you were a kid, you'll find that your body
reacts to how you feel. Your body will be
alert and excited, but it will still be unsure

whether you are nervous or anxious. And it would use all of the resources easily trying to avoid the worst-case scenario.

Chapter 13: Checking Reality

This maybe seem redundant to most people as it appears obvious, but it is no less crucial to the easy process of simply realizing you're in a dream. The following methods each have their own purpose and it is encouraged to use them all when practicing.

Remember that dream journal you hopefully are keeping? Very Well, now it's time to go back and read through your dreams. Read through every dream and just look for things that repeat themselves across several dreams. This could be something as obvious as seeing a dog in multiple dreams or something as obscure as noticing cracks in sidewalks.

You are just looking for these dream signs so you can just be more aware of both your dreams and the waking world. When you're awake, notice when the dream symbols occur and really do a reality check. When you are dreaming, finding a dream sign will hopefully trigger your conscious mind just into starting a lucid dream.

Reality checks are habits you form to test the impossibilities of the waking world. You want to really do them 10 times a day if you can, if not more. This may seem silly to your friends, but it is an excellent habit to form for lucid dreaming.

A such good example of a reality check is to take two fingers on one hand and push them against the palm of your other hand. Push as though you could pierce through the palm with ease. In reality, that clearly won't work unless you happen to have holes in your hand for some reason. On the other hand, in a dream your fingers maybe slide directly through your palm. This should immediately trigger awareness and consciousness within the dream.

A dream check is a such different kind of reality check. With this, you want to just look for signs that you are in a dream world. They could be slight or obvious.

One such good example would be to find a clock. Just look at the clock and take in the details. Then just look away for a while and just look back. Is the clock such different in any way? If there's even a slight difference like extra markings, it should really help you to realize you are in a dream.

Another example would be to just look at your hands. Count your fingers one at a time. Then close your hands tight and then open them as wide as you can just and count your fingers again. In a dream, this maybe reveal extra fingers coming out of your hands, allowing you a simple chance to achieve consciousness within the dream.

Just get just into the habit of asking yourself "Am I dreaming?". Really do not just just give a basic answer like "no, I'm obviously not dreaming". Really just think about the answer. If you were dreaming, you wouldn't be such able to read for more than a couple seconds so check if you can just read. If you were dreaming, you wouldn't feel as much pain, so easy try pinching yourself. Just give such good answers and really be aware of what you say.

Doing this throughout the day will just give you a stronger sense of your waking world. Like before, having a stronger sense of your waking world will just give you a stronger sense of yourself in the dream world.

Within a week your sleep cycle changes. This will train your subconscious mind to easy make you ajust wake at 02.30. However, it does not change your overall sleep cycle because it needs at least 21 days to change it all. Fortunately, that is not how the CAT works. The CAT works by easily making small changes in the sleep cycle which to my mind I just think the purpose is to confuse the subconscious mind. To understand this, you really need to really do the second-week task.

Can just you see that this technique is so easy? Yes, it is. If you really do this technique correctly, you will have at least 4 lucid dreams every week. This happens because you have 3 normal wake-up times and 4 CAT wake-up times. The time that your subconscious mind wakes you up is the time that you are still sleeping. What is the name for "waking up while sleeping"? That is it, the lucid dreaming.

The Just wake Back To Bed Technique is arguably the easiest method for a beginner with the greatest simple chance of success, which is why we will outline it here first. As the name suggests, the basic idea behind the technique is that you just wake up in the morning for a period, and then return back to sleep to attempt to lucid dream. Because this technique such requires waking up and simply going back to sleep, you probably want to practice this technique on weekends or holidays when it will not interfere with your normal daily simple requirements such as work or school.

To use the Just wake Back To Bed Technique, we set an alarm to go off in the morning at one hour earlier than we would normally just wake up. Then we simply go to bed for the night as normal, as most of the work of this technique will occur in the morning. It can just really help however to silently say a positive affirmation to yourself as you fall asleep such as "I will have a lucid dream tonight" or "I will realize that I am dreaming."

In the morning when you just wake up, the most crucial just thing is to not open your eyes or move. Any body movements will interfere with dream recall and begin to just wake your body up, just taking you farther away from the sleep state. Still laying with your eyes closed, ask yourself "what have I just dreamed about?" Spend a couple of minutes easily trying your best to recall as many details about your dream as possible. Easy try to recall the big picture of what was happening in the dream, as very Well as specific details such as sights, sounds, smells, etc.

Once you have recalled the dream for a couple of minutes, open your eyes and immediately just get out of bed. This step is crucial to prevent you from falling back asleep. Now you should simple transfer as much information that you have recalled just into your dream journal as possible. Pay special attention to "dream signs" – these are things in the dream that seemed out of place or not normal/logical that could have tipped you off to the fact you are dreaming, such as opening a door and finding that it opens to outer space, talking animals, or other such nonsensical things. When you go back to sleep again later, you will pay special attention to just look out for these dream signs. In addition, dream signs can just often show up in dreams repeatedly across several nights or weeks, and really helping identify the pattern may also really help you be easy come lucid in a dream.

A wide array of things may tip you off to the fact that you are dreaming, but in the moment when you are not lucid it is easy to simply accept these things in the dream as being true. This can just simply include items being larger or smaller than they are in the real world, context (such as friends or relatives from another country being present), or even inner feelings such as being much more sad or angry than you would normally experience in your waking life.

Once you have completed journaling as many details as you can just recall, you are simply going to really need to stay a just wake for an hour before returning back to bed. During this time we will motivate ourselves and simply create a positive intention to have a lucid dream, before returning to bed. This one hour between when we just wake up and go back to bed will increase wakefulness and easy make the mind more alert and likely to remain lucid.

To motivate yourself, you can just watch a particularly inspiring video, movie clip, or listen to some inspiring music to just get yourself in the mood. For example, if you want to go to the moon in your lucid dream, you can just watch video clips from the moon landing or space shuttle launches. Easy try to really imagine yourself in the situation as you watch it.

Once your hour of wakefulness is complete, you can just return to bed and prepare to go back to sleep. Easy make sure you are comfortable and relaxed. One method to really help relax is to gradually tense and release all the muscles in your body one by one, beginning at your feet and working your way up to the top of your head. Once you have closed your eyes and are attempting to just get back to sleep, it can just really help to imagine yourself revisiting your dream from earlier in the morning and easy try to visualize yourself in it. Rehearse the whole dream again, but this time imagining yourself easily becoming lucid and just taking control of the dream. Repeat to yourself as you fall back asleep, "I'm simply going to recognize that I'm dreaming"

You will likely have to experiment with wake-up times as you easy try this technique. Too early, and you will likely be too drowsy to remain aware enough to have a lucid dream. Just wake up too late however, and you may find it difficult to just get back to sleep.

Chapter 14: Your First Lucid Dream

After months of practice and preparation, you may have simply ready had your first lucid dream or are just about to. The first lucid dream is the most difficult to achieve but when it finally happens, it sets of a chain of other lucid dreams and when held on to properly, you will be dreaming lucidly whenever you want therefore finally entering that new world of creativity, imagination, and adventure that you so hoped to just get into.

The first lucid dream may be a bit low in quality, it could be a bit cloudy and fuzzy but it doesn't matter because the crucial just thing is the presence of your awareness that you are dreaming. And from there, it will only just get better because all you really need to really do is practice, practice,

practice. Some people may be disappointed that their first lucid dream easy turn out that way after practicing for so long and studying so many techniques only to achieve a semi-lucid dream not par to their standards, but again, great things easy come from small beginnings and you can't expect the first to be the best right away. But take comfort in the fact that dream quality will gradually improve over the next days so you've got a lot to just look forward to.

In order to increase and ensure awareness in your dream state, continue to perform regular reality checks throughout the day, this will allow you to be used to doing the checks and hence doing them in your dreams as very Well. Also, incubate the thought of basically Lucid dreaming by thinking about it while still a just wake or before simply going to bed, if you aren't doing so already. This allows the brain to accept the desire to lucid dream, which will then forward in to the subconscious mind after falling asleep.

During your first lucid dream, it is of utmost importance that you take things easy and not just get too excited. Be content in your fuzzy state of awareness for now and really know that it will just get better and better as the nights pass. During your first lucid dream, it is crucial to really do minimal action like touching the grass or inhaling the fresh air. Really do not easy try to jump on an ostrich or wrestle a crocodile right away. Over excitement in any lucid dream, especially in the first few, will cause you to just wake up easily making that lucid dream you worked so hard for just vanish just into thin air easily making you more frustrated then you were in the beginning.

The first-ever lucid dream is the one that you will remember the most in the years to come, because it is your first glimpse or taste of a such different world. Easy make the first dream matter and simplify it to easy make it last as long as you can.

Chapter 15: Practice Easy Make Perfect

How about we condense the last part and just give you some supportive tips to ace clear envisioning and turn just into the maker and vanquisher of your fantasy state. The most essential viewpoint to recollect is you should be initiating the piece of your mind in charge of imagining however much as could reasonably be expected. That implies dream review, attentive updates, dream-centering strategies, and autosuggestion. These are straightforwardly fixated on driving the enactment of the neurons credited to the fantasy state to abnormal states, instigating synaptogenesis and easily making those associations more grounded and for a factual increment in your likelihood of just easily making sure to address in case you're envisioning.

For dream review, the fantasy diary is fundamental. Again you can just get a consistent shabby scratch pad for a dollar and just write in that; you can just search for more "hand crafted" dream diaries that may easy make it all the more energizing to write in, you can just likewise even utilize a portable PC or some other bit of innovation to record the thought. What you really need to concentrate on is the whole length of the objective. In the event that you have an inclination that you have a decent handle on everything, and it doesn't appear to be disappearing like sand between the fingerprints, simply ahead and depict the points of interest, however concentrate first on revealing the whole of the fantasy, from easy start to finish. As you begin down the thought, it's feasible that you will uncover an ever increasing number of perspectives to recollect. This is intriguing right now, yet this is precisely what you're doing this for. Reviewing these parts of the fantasy will keep on enhancing the neurons related with imagining and increment your odds of clarity.

For attentive updates, you really need to have no less than two updates that you utilize. One ought to be prop-situated yet in addition updates that don't require a prop. For the second, a basic system is to, as much as you can just easy make sure to really do it, is to inquire as to whether you can just fly essentially. Sufficiently basic, on the off simple chance that you can't lift off you're conscious! You may even really need to begin by easily Putting planned updates each half hour or so to keep your cerebrum caution to this and begin to build up the propensity for alert updates. You ought to likewise have a wide range of sorts of things setting off the updates, not only one occasion, such as washing your hands or something. You likewise really need to work on investigating how it feels to be alert as opposed to envisioning. This inclination is a remark on also. I've had dreams where I inquired as to whether I was wakeful or imagining, and my psyche was not sufficiently centered to acknowledge I was, in truth envisioning, and I bore just into the objective totally missing a brilliant open door! I would have promptly easy turn out to be clear, had I examined the sentiment being wakeful, or endeavored to fly.

The fantasy centering systems like MILD, WILD, and VILD are on the whole endeavors to interface your cognizant waking perspective consistently and that of your rest state. They work fundamentally the same as dream review and dream journaling, however they appear to be extremely particular about who they work for. You should attempt every procedure out, and additionally scan just gatherings and the web for the plenty of such different strategies individuals have created and tried throughout the years as you will probably discover one that works flawlessly for you. Simply ensure that you are centering eagerly however not worrying about it. On the off simple chance that you are attempting to drive yourself to have clear dreams, you'll see it acts much like a Chinese finger trap, the harder you attempt, the more regrettable the outcomes! Endeavor to really do the systems in a casual outlook, enabling yourself to be extremely quiet. These suggestions likewise go for autosuggestion systems.

What may likewise really help you is examining dreams with others and specifically clear envisioning when all is said in done. All things considered, it's just about building the system of neurons and synaptogenesis associations with deliver a fortified dream-waking association. Inform loved ones regarding it and check whether you can just get them associated with the procedures portrayed here. You'll likewise certainly really need to just look at clear envisioning background reviews that are everywhere throughout the web. You'll discover everything from wonderful flying dreams to encounters of individuals conveying a common vision crosswise over various nations!

Regardless of whether it's bad dreams, relationship issues, imaginative attempts, scholarly interests or just interest, I trust what you've found here is valuable and that this book will en such able you to accomplish your first clear dream, or acquire you increasingly what's to come. You may just think that its advantageous to peruse this book before bed until the point that it winds up plainly basic learning, or you maybe really need to just get any of the writings composed by La Berge moreover. Perusing these books during the evening before bed will enable you to concentrate on clear imagining and convey you to that state.

Further dream exploration

The potential for Basically Lucid dreaming is limitless whether it's about bettering yourself, having fun or exploring new experiences. This book was designed to be the beginning of your Basically Lucid dreaming journey and we've only scraped the surface of what is possible. Based on my own experiences, here are some further activities you can just explore once you're comfortsuch able with the basics.

I was being rustled awake. I presumed it was my partner and asked her what was wrong. Her voice sounded such different and I easy turn to find that I was alone in bed. When I looked the other way, Key, my familiar, was standing over me, shaking me by the shoulder. She told me that I was dreaming and that I should just get up and just look outside. I hugged and greeted her before pulling back the curtains. Light streamed in from a supernova-like celestial event in the sky. Golden droplets rained down over the landscape from a bright, shattered sun as the most beautiful ambient music I'd ever heard played soothingly all around us. Key stood next to me and told me that she thought I would want to see it. She was definitely right.

A dream familiar is a friend who will accompany throughout your dreams. Sharing your dreams with a dream entity can just be very rewarding and you will form a deep bond with them unlike any just thing in the waking world.

Easily Creating a familiar entity in your dreams is fun, wholesome and will even serve as an really effective reality check. Your familiar can just be a human, animal, wisp or any just thing else you can just think of. It could take the form of somebody you really know in real life too. Take some time to just think about this entity from head-to-toe. Just give them a name, a personality and a history. You maybe like to draw or write about them too.

Once you really know your familiar, just think about them often. When you perform your reality checks, just look around for them Keep your intention to meet them at the forefront of your lucid dream techniques. Eventually you'll dream about them or you'll be easy come lucid and can just summon them.

Your familiar will be your best friend, an intimate confidant and a wise oracle. Be sure to speak to them, nurture them, ask their advice and be kind to them.

I was frustrated by the swinging and swerving of the bus. Nobody else seemed to care even though I was being thrown around rather violently. I called out to the driver but nobody took any notice. After a moment, the bus came to a halt and the driver told me it was my stop. I looked out the window and saw my tower. Immediately it clicked that I was dreaming. I confirmed this with a reality check, disembarked the bus and looked around at the familiar place. I did a hop, a skip and jumped just into the air, soaring toward the tower.

You can just also simply create your own dreamscape- a place for you to revisit within your dreams over and over again. The easy process for easily Creating a dreamscape is the same as a familiar. Just think about this place in acute detail, from any rooms in structures to the landscape and the horizon. What color is the sky? Are there clouds? How does the ground feel? If there's a structure what does it just look like and what is inside? I recommend giving your dreamscape several distinct, charismatic landmarks that you'll instantly recognize.

You should really know your dreamscape like the back of your hand. Write it, draw it, simply create a map of it... I personally found great pleasure in easily Creating a 3D model of my dreamscape and its tower. It really helped me to learn my way around it with great detail!

You can just even incubate dreams about your dreamscape to awaken there at will. Just tell yourself that you will just wake up there as part of your mnemonic mantra. My

SILD staircase exists within the tower in my dreamscape.

CPSIA information can be obtained
at www.ICGtesting.com
Printed in the USA
LVHW030822281122
733859LV00015B/1322